Lancashire Railw

on old picture po

Norman Ellis

S 2551 LONDON ROAD STATION, MANCHESTER.

1. The approach to **Manchester London Road** station is splendidly illustrated on this W.H. Smith 'Kingsway' series card, posted to Whitehaven in 1908. The station's Italianate façade, dating from 1866, was designed by local architects Mills & Murgatroyd. Various rail companies used the station, including the L&NW. To the left is the same company's goods station and warehouse.

£3.95

Introduction

A Kodak box camera faithfully recorded much of my childhood. There I am in 1931, on the beach at Blackpool, not quite two years old. Mother and father are on some of the snaps. So is grandma, dressed in sombre dark clothes, black stockings and a huge black hat. We were at Blackpool for the annual Wakefield holiday week, having travelled by train from the city's Kirkgate station. That was my first experience of the seaside. It was also a first for grandma. I don't think she enjoyed the experience and never went again. In future years, when we holidayed at Blackpool or Scarborough, we left her with other family members. At Blackpool, we stayed at a small guest house, which provided 'apartment' accommodation, meaning that we purchased most of our own food, placed it in an allotted space in a cupboard and let the landlady cook it for us where necessary. The 'lounge' was a threadbare sofa at the edge of the dining area. You were not expected to hang about after meals.

In the early 1930s, there were still guest houses whose bedrooms had no running hot or cold water. In such cases, the bedroom was supplied with a bowl-full of warm water for the early morning wash. But by the late 1930s, an increasing number of guest houses boasted running hot and cold water and electric light in bedrooms. Even a bathroom was sometimes mentioned.

The Holidays with Pay Act of 1938 brought one week's paid holiday for an increasing number of workers, whose families had relied heavily on savings clubs and the dividend from the Co-op. But from 1939, traditional holidays were jeopardised because of the War. Afterwards, the holiday scene was set for change, with Rail Nationalisation in 1947, increased coach travel in the 1950s, and the subsequent emergence of family cars.

Consequent upon the Industrial Revolution, there had been increasing dissatisfaction in many parts of Britain with the conveyance of goods by road and canal. As a direct result, the Liverpool to Manchester Railway was conceived in the 1820s. Although not the first railway in the land, the L&M established a precedent in 1830 by using locomotive engines throughout its length and taking seriously the carriage of passengers. But the conveyance of goods, particularly cotton, was at its heart.

The southern and eastern regions of Lancashire had plentiful supplies of rain-water and good proximity to coal seams. These were ideal requirements for the cotton industry which eventually evolved on a massive scale. Manchester became the commercial hub of the cotton activity, with Liverpool the major port, where raw cotton was imported and finished goods exported. The areas north of Preston and the Ribble Valley, well away from the industrial towns further south, offered less incentive to the rail companies, although the London & North Western pushed a line through to Carlisle, via Lancaster and Carnforth. From Carnforth, the Furness Railway provided a gateway to the shores of Morecambe Bay and parts of the Lake District.

Picture postcards were first published in Britain in 1894, but it was not until a decade later that they began to take off, when in 1902 the Post Office allowed a message to be written on the address side. This meant that the whole of one side was available for the picture and obviously gave more scope to publishers. Photographic viewcards became very popular, and the postcard became the most important way of communicating news or messages, in much the same way as the telephone is used today. The years up to 1914 were the 'Golden Age' of picture postcards, when millions of imaginative designs covering every subject under the sun were published by a host of national and local firms. Railway stations were favoured locations for postcard views, though coverage was haphazard. Those featured in this book are from my collection. If your local station hasn't been included, it may well be that no old postcards of it exist.

Where known, the name of the publisher of a postcard is mentioned, but many were published anonymously.

Norman Ellis
July 2011

S.17958.   LONDON ROAD STATION, MANCHESTER.

2. Around thirty years later, W.H. Smith issued another postcard showing the façade of **Manchester London Road** station, with crowds of people striding to catch their trains. The station had passed into London, Midland & Scottish and London & North Eastern Railway ownership. In September 1960, it became known as Manchester Piccadilly, after extensive rebuilding. The structure at extreme right is the old fire station on London Road.

Front cover: This irrecoverable scene of **Heysham Harbour** station from c.1906 extols the days of steam and sail. The station was opened by the Midland Railway in 1904 for its Belfast and Isle of Man boats. The building's overall ridge-and-furrow roof was supported by steel members, but timber was mainly used for the platforms and individual buildings. This station was closed in 1970 and replaced by another one further east.

Back cover (top): **Langho** station, on the L&Y line from Blackburn to Hellifield, typified the country station at its best. The name of the village is Saxon and thought to derive from the Battle of Billangho, fought here in AD 798. The larger buildings on the right, including a station house, were complemented by a simple shelter on the left. Langho is much expanded today, but it had lost its passenger station by 1956. The card was issued by J.W. Shaw of Blackburn in the 'West End' series.

Back cover (bottom): **Old Trafford** station was Manchester's cricket ground station, and a hive of activity even as far back as May 1887 when the Royal Jubilee Exhibition was held there. The message on the back includes the comment " *It is rotten up here, no fine weather, all wet day and night.*" The station was on the Manchester South Junction & Altrincham Railway, which remained largely independent for most of its life. Bowns of Old Trafford issued the card.

Railway Stations

By the 1870s, Britain's railway network was almost complete, with Lancashire having one of the greatest concentrations of lines. Several large railway companies, and some lesser ones, brought their expertise to the region. Whilst they mostly set their sights on goods traffic, they were mindful of the passenger potential and built railway stations accordingly. The cities and larger towns usually acquired more than one station.

Although most railway stations incorporated the same basic features, there were degrees of individuality. Overall form and size depended on location, availability of building materials and the architect's whim. Village stations usually had a booking hall, waiting rooms, toilets, a goods office and possibly a stationmaster's house. Frequently, all these features were housed in buildings on one platform, the other platform merely having a passenger shelter. Bigger stations incorporated the same basic components, sometimes repeated on several platforms. Refreshment rooms, bookstalls and administrative offices were additional features. A concourse or overall roof added a touch of luxury, as did an attractive exterior.

Whilst railway stations were capable of creating an aura of glamour for passengers, the same cannot be said of the sections dealing with the merchandise. Sidings, goods sheds and loading bays were often located adjacent to the smaller stations. In industrial towns, these features were more extensive and took up space away from the passenger facilities. Although station architecture has been well studied, it has never been properly appreciated. Unique stations have been neglected or lost.

Cotton Towns and Wakes Weeks

The coming of cotton and the spread of railways brought a fresh impetus and identity to the towns of east and south Lancashire. Mills with tall belching chimneys, rows of workers' houses, the knocker-up, the early morning clatter of clogs – these were symbols of a new prosperity, at least for some. Surrounding villages received their own railway station. But by 1900, tram travel was becoming a viable alternative to train journeying.

Out of all this the annual Wakes Week experience was born, when each town shut down its mills and factories. The fixed dates occurred any time between late June and early September. A day or two at the seaside by train, or in the country by tramcar, may have become, by the 1920s and 1930s, a week-long holiday at Blackpool, Morecambe or Southport. On Saturday mornings, stations were throng with parents and children, with luggage, buckets and spades. The railway companies coped marvellously with this increased traffic on a relatively few days of the year. Many Yorkshire people also travelled to the Lancashire coast on their annual Feast Week.

Principal Railway Companies in Lancashire

Cheshire Lines Committee (CLC). This was the joint property of the Great Central, Great Northern and Midland, with each part of the trio nominating three of their directors to represent them on the board (the Committee). Its operations were in south Lancashire and north Cheshire.

Lancashire & Yorkshire Railway (L&Y). Incorporated in 1847, it was already an amalgam of several companies, chief of which was the Manchester & Leeds. From Liverpool in the west to Goole in the east, it covered many of the industrial areas of Lancashire and Yorkshire.

London & North Western Railway (L&NW). It was formed in 1846 by amalgamation of several important railways, including the Liverpool & Manchester. Its influence stretched from Carlisle to London Euston via Birmingham, with inroads into Wales and Lancashire.

Midland Railway (MR). Formed in 1844 by an amalgam of three previous railways, it became, through gradual expansion, a driving influence in parts of central and northern England. St Pancras was its London terminus. Its Heysham Harbour complex, opened in 1904, was a relatively late addition.

Furness Railway (FR). Starting life as a mineral railway around Barrow, the passenger and tourist potential of the area was soon recognised. Rail extensions were made to Carnforth, Lakeside (Windermere) and Coniston. Its steamers plied from Barrow to Belfast and Fleetwood.

S 2542   CENTRAL STATION, MANCHESTER.

3. Manchester Central station, belonging to the Cheshire Lines Railway, is pictured on a WHS 'Kingsway' card posted in 1908. The frontage shows the names of the other participating companies, although the Midland reference is hidden by the veranda. The arched roof covered six platforms.

61697.   MANCHESTER CENTRAL STATION.

4. This is **Manchester Central** station, probably c.1939, after the 1923 Grouping, which is reflected in the revised names above the entrance. Who remembers *Picture Post*, the famous illustrated weekly magazine? The overall roof proved useful when the station was eventually converted to an exhibition centre. The card was published by C. Richter of London.

5. Opened in 1900, and photographed a few years later, the Midland Hotel, Manchester, was situated opposite Central station. A veranda, shown on the left, crossed Windmill Street and connected the station with the hotel. This was regarded as the city's most prestigious hotel.

6. The London & North Western Railway opened **Manchester Exchange** station in 1884. It was actually a western extension to Victoria station (off the picture to the right) which the L&NW had shared with the L&Y. The card, published by Valentine of Dundee, was posted in 1941, by which year the station was in LMS ownership.

7. The approach to **Manchester Exchange** station, viewed here c.1905, crossed the River Irwell. Close proximity to the Cotton Exchange gave the station its name. It was closed on 5 May 1969. The postcard comes from A&G Taylor of 62 Market Street, Manchester, in their 'Reality' series.

8. Signalman Smith is photographed at the lever frame of **Manchester Exchange** station's no. 2 signal box in March 1910. The continuous platform constructed between Victoria and Exchange was reputed to be the longest station platform in Britain.

9. Manchester Victoria station was opened in 1844. By the early 1900s, and following various spates of rebuilding, and as the headquarters of the L&Y, it was handling 700 trains a day. Here, the main concourse is shown, c.1910, on a Valentine's 'XL' series postcard. Nobody, it seems, had a good word for the building's exterior.

10. The *Daily Sketch* (published in London and Manchester) photographed these recruits at **Manchester Victoria** station on 17 February 1917. Jessie Sutton and another young lady on the left were serving them coffee and wishing them luck.

S 9381   EXCHANGE STATION, LIVERPOOL.

11. Liverpool Exchange station was opened by the Lancashire & Yorkshire Railway in 1850. Extensive rebuilding in 1884-8 produced the façade shown, behind whose walls was the station hotel. The station lost most of its services in 1977. The WHS 'Kingsway' card was posted in 1912.

12. The scene is **Liverpool Exchange** station, probably in 1911, when the card was posted. The extensive docks at Fleetwood, specially adapted for fish and timber, were part property of the L&Y. Therefore, the promotion of fish at Liverpool is not surprising. Express services of fish trains ran to Birmingham, London and Scotland.

13. Liverpool Lime Street station formed the eventual completion of the pioneer Liverpool & Manchester Railway. It was built in a noble part of the city by the London & North Western Railway. Here, the huge station complex, with its glazed roofs, is partly hidden by the magnificent façade of the station hotel.

14. The Cheshire Lines Committee opened their **Liverpool Central** station in 1874. When closed in 1972, the site was developed as Ranelagh Street shopping centre. Part of the station frontage is shown on the right, with erstwhile Lewis's beyond. The Mersey Railway continued to operate from here at deeper levels.

RIVERSIDE STATION, LIVERPOOL.

15. Liverpool Riverside station, of the Mersey Docks & Harbour Board, was constructed near Prince's landing stage, where Atlantic liners moored for embarkation and landing of passengers. Horse brakes stand ready, c.1910, to convey passengers to other Liverpool stations. The foremost carries White Star Line identity.

16. This horse brake, belonging to the London & North Western Railway (and pictured on an L&NW officially-issued card of 1905) shuttled people between Liverpool Lime Street station and Isle of Man steamers.

17. 'Dimples' posted this card from Warrington to Yarm-on-Tees on 20 January 1905 with the message, "*I will write tomorrow. Is not this view good?*" It shows Horsemarket Street, Warrington, looking towards the Cheshire Lines Committee's **Warrington Central** station, in an elevated position on the right.

18. Boys look on as a motley collection of characters wait on **Urmston** station, c.1910, for the next train to Manchester, six miles away to the east. With long awnings covering the platforms, the CLC obviously did not want passengers to get wet whilst waiting. J Wride of Flixton Road produced the card.

19. The Liverpool, Crosby & Southport Railway opened a line from Liverpool to Southport in 1848. The Lancashire & Yorkshire took over in 1855. On this line, **Blundellsands & Crosby** station served Blundellsands, Little Crosby and Great Crosby. The station looks well-equipped. Of particular interest is the public telephone box at extreme right. The card was posted in 1913.

20. The L&Y station staff, including the stationmaster (and a dog) pose for the camera on **Walton Junction** station, on the northern outskirts of Liverpool. The station approach was behind the buildings on the right. The card has a squared-circle postmark for Rice Lane, Liverpool, dated 15 June 1905.

21. The large town of Rochdale became famous for cotton, wool - and the Rochdale Pioneers. The L&Y provided this splendid **Rochdale** station in 1889, replacing an earlier one slightly further north. Its allure diminished when the clock tower was removed. The whole façade was replaced in 1980. The card was published by Thomas Pinder, photo artist, Rochdale.

22. Fine steelwork and capacious canopies characterised the interior of **Rochdale** station, noted for its many platforms, bays, cavernous subways and platform facilities. Today, the station interior is much altered. Reaching the station involved a stiff climb from the town centre. Both these views date from c.1907.

23. At **Castleton** station, a cluster of well-dressed people await the arrival of an L&Y train from Rochdale (two miles away) on its way to Manchester Victoria, c.1905. The Lanky's nearby sidings served a cotton machine manufacturer and a maltsters.

24. The Parish Church of St. Thomas, in decorated style, overlooks the more worldly **New Hey** station, on the L&Y route from Rochdale to Oldham. Behind the simple but adequate-looking station, photographed c.1905, goods sidings are visible.

COPYRIGHT
RBM. 2

BRIDGE STREET. RAMSBOTTOM

LILYWHITE LTD
BRIGHOUSE

25. The road and rail activities on Bridge Street were controlled by **Ramsbottom** station signal box on the right, the station being on the left. The former L&Y station was closed to goods in 1966 and passengers in 1972. The card was published by Lilywhite of Brighouse in the 1930s.

26. The main building (in stone) on **Lower Darwen** station, on the L&Y line between Blackburn and Bolton, resembled a Georgian style house. The awning, although useful, looks incongruous. Like Darwen, its larger neighbour, Lower Darwen had cotton spinning. The card was posted from Darwen to Blackburn in 1904. The station closed in 1958.

27. The railwayana on Station Road, **Hoghton**, includes a signal cabin, level crossing gates, signal and footbridge. The latter was located at the end of Hoghton station, off the picture, right. The building further up the road is the station hotel. The village's claim to fame is Hoghton Tower, a 16th century fortified mansion.

28. Hoghton signal box was to a fairly standard L&Y design, with brick base. After 1886, the company obtained signalling equipment from its new works at Horwich. Both these cards date from c.1907. The station, on the line from Preston to Blackburn, closed to passengers in 1960.

29. Burnley was the centre of cotton weaving, but its other trades included cotton s
stations, the one near the infantry barracks, called **Burnley Barracks** station, catered t
were 31/6d each! At Burnley Wakes, and other holiday times too, the station becam

dyeing and bleaching, textile engineering, coal mining and brick making. Of its two
passengers than freight. Part of this L&Y station is shown when Beaty Brothers suits
isy.

30. Holme station was situated on the 'Copy Pit' line of the L&Y, constructed in 1849 to connect Burnley with Todmorden. All the line's intermediate stations had closed by 1961, Holme shutting in 1930. A crossover track is visible on this view. The line now forms part of a picturesque route from Bradford to Blackpool.

31. The L&Y came to **Appley Bridge**, on its line from Wigan to Southport, and appropriated some of the freight business from the Leeds & Liverpool Canal, which flowed through the village. This included stone, brick tiles, coal and flour. The scene covers the passenger and freight facilities at the station.

32. Standish station stood on the London & North Western line north of Wigan. *"You will find our railway station is a very small one."* So wrote Lucy when she posted the card. Timber structures, as instanced here, were often favoured by the L&NW. Notices advise passengers to cross the line by the underbridge. The station closed in 1949.

WALKDEN STATION.   No 1089.

33. Walkden was served by two stations. This one was on the L&NW line from Manchester Exchange to Bolton. The neat station, with floral embellishments, was approached from four sloping footways. It lost its regular passenger service in 1954. The card, by Charles Wilkinson of Manchester, was posted in 1930.

34. Morecambe Euston Road station was opened by the L&NW in 1886. Its yellow brick used to gleam in the sunshine. As well as five passenger platforms, there were excellent freight facilities, including cattle pens and coal wharves. From 1958, the station only opened in summer; it shut completely in 1962. The card, by B. Matthews of Bradford, was used in 1922.

35. On 17 September 1912, whilst crossing from the fast to the slow lane at **Ditton** station (near Widnes), the entire 5.30 pm express from Chester to Liverpool was derailed. Fifteen people were killed and fifty injured. Driver inexperience was the cause. Here, the mangled L&NW 2-4-0 is being manoeuvred after the accident.

36. Blackpool Talbot Road station, shown c.1905, was built by the Preston & Wyre Railway, and eventually came under joint L&Y and L&NW ownership. Its twin-arched overall roof covered seven platforms, with eight excursion platforms outside. The station was extensively rebuilt in 1974. The card was published by John Walker, London, in the 'Bells' series.

37. Part of the twin-arched trainshed at **Blackpool Talbot Road** station is pictured during a royal reception, on a card posted in May 1912. The station was renamed Blackpool North in 1932. This part of the station was cleared in 1974 to build a supermarket. The new station was built on the site of the excursion platforms.

38. Blackpool Central station, of P&W origin, was also operated by the L&Y and L&NW. It became especially important for its day excursion arrivals in LMS and BR days, with four hundred or more passengers disgorging from each train. This happy group (perhaps a club) look set for enjoyment. The station closed in 1964.

39. The Carnival King and Queen are seen arriving at **Blackpool South Shore** station (LMS) in June 1924, before parading along the promenade in procession. This second of what was planned to be an annual event was not repeated because of rowdyism.

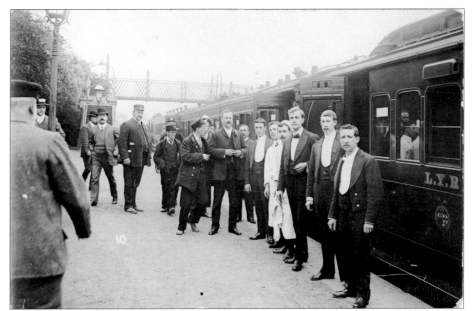

40. Excitement prevails at **Blackpool Waterloo Road** station. L&Y employees, including restaurant car staff, feature beside a train of company carriages. The station, on the Preston & Wyre line from Kirkham to Blackpool, was jointly operated by the L&Y and L&NW. It was eventually integrated with Blackpool South station.

41. Fleetwood station, extreme right, became a joint enterprise of the L&Y and L&NW. The large station complex provided access from trains to steamers for Belfast and the Isle of Man. According to a sign, electric cars (trams) ran to and from Blackpool every few minutes. The card was posted in 1915.

42. Trains came to Leyland in 1838, courtesy of the North Union Railway, whose successors were the L&NW and L&Y. **Leyland** station is shown c.1910. The structures on the left-hand platform (off picture) were of NU origin. The timber buildings on the island and other platform are of L&NW design. The town became famous for Leyland Motors.

43. This sturdy stone structure stood at **Brinscall** station on the Lancashire Union Railway (later L&Y and L&NW joint). Railway sidings were constructed to quarries, cotton mills and paper mills in the area. The card was posted to nearby Chorley in 1905. The station lost its passenger service in 1960.

44. A permanent-way gang pauses for a photograph at Dewsnap Sidings signal box, just east of **Guide Bridge**, in 1905 or thereabouts. The cabin, of Great Central Railway design and with nineteen working levers, was brought into use in 1905 to control a number of new and busy junctions.

45. Part of the **Manchester London Road** station complex was used by the Great Central Railway goods department, where employees are shown posed beside their horse and steam wagons, c.1912. The building on the right was a grain and flour warehouse. The steam lorries were built by Hercules of Levenshulme.

46. The Midland Railway station at **Didsbury** added opulence to the area. Some of Manchester's affluent merchants made their homes in this pleasant city suburb. The clock tower was erected in memory of Dr Milson Rhodes, a local benefactor. The station closed in 1969 and was demolished in 1981. The card was posted in 1911.

47. The neat **Heaton Mersey** station was similar to that at Didsbury on the same stretch of Midland line (a standardisation trait often pursued by a railway company). There are fancy bargeboards to the roof gables, interesting adverts and a seated (mostly) group of station staff. The line and station closed in 1969.

S 2428   MIDLAND RAILWAY STATION, MORECAMBE.

48. After inheriting the (Little) North Western station on Morecambe jetty, the Midland superseded it with the new **Morecambe Promenade** station in 1907. It boasted four platforms 300 yards long, and a huge 'circulating area.' This is shown on the WHS 'Kingsway' card. There are hanging baskets galore and some huge lavatory signs.

1039 HEYSHAM HARBOUR.

49. Heysham Harbour station was opened by the MR in 1904 for its Belfast and Isle of Man steamers. From 1898, a new railway from Morecambe accessed the site and enabled work to commence. The area was excavated, then flooded, and enclosed by two huge breakwaters. Here, construction work is well advanced.

50. The Midland's **Lancaster Green Ayre** station was built in Gothic style to contrast with the Tudor styling at Lancaster Castle station. It was opened in 1900 and electrified in 1908. Here, subsequent work is in hand on the junction at the station's western end. Passenger services were withdrawn in 1966.

51. The complex layout of lines, points and electric gantries is emphasised on this view in the vicinity of **Lancaster Castle** station, probably c.1908. Lines hereabouts were used by the L&NW and MR. Although the station is off the picture, left, the goods and grain warehouse of the MR is visible, centre.

52. This Midland line along the Lune Valley from Lancaster was axed in the early 1960s. Bob posted the card from Caton in 1912 and praised the scenery thereabouts. **Caton** station, with its timber and plaster effects, looks equally impressive. There were cotton and bobbin-making mills in the vicinity.

S 7545   PRESTON STATION, NO. 9 PLATFORM.

53. The enlarged and improved **Preston** station came into use in 1880 and is shown about thirty years later on a WHS 'Kingsway' card, which may have been purchased from the station bookshop on platform 9. The busy station was used by L&Y and L&NW trains to the Fylde, and was the latter's gateway to Cumberland.

CARNFORTH STATION.

54. **Carnforth** was famous for its iron foundries. It became an important rail centre for those wishing to visit the Lakes or the area around Morecambe Bay. On this postcard of Carnforth station by Sankey of Barrow, c.1914, the Furness Railway platforms are on the left, with those of the L&NW on the right. A Weyman bookstall is visible.

Station, Grange-over-Sands.

55. As a quieter alternative to Morecambe across the bay, the Furness Railway promoted Grange-over-Sands and laid out its park and ornamental lake. The charming **Grange-over-Sands** station is shown on a card by H.K. Duckworth, a chemist in Grange. Without doubt, the railway brought a burgeoning prosperity to the area.

S.Y. "SWIFT" AT LAKE SIDE PIER, (WINDERMERE)   COPYRIGHT

56. To promote the Lakeland tourist area, the Furness Railway issued a number of official postcards, including this one of the steam yacht 'Swift' at **Windermere Lakeside** station. The boat was built for the FR in 1900, to carry 700 passengers. The card was published by Raphael Tuck of London, the top postcard firm of the first half of the 20th century.

3791   CENTRAL STATION, BARROW.   SANKEYS

57. A Swiss chalet-type of architecture much favoured by the Furness Railway reached a peak with the construction of the new **Barrow-in-Furness Central** station in 1882. A London train is being hauled by a pair of 4-4-0 locomotives in about 1913. The Barrow firm of Sankey published the card.

58. The L&NW opened a branch from Lancaster to Glasson Dock in 1883. This wooden structure on **Glasson Dock** station housed a booking hall, waiting room and toilets. Facilities at the station ended in 1930 (passengers) and 1964 (freight). The quayside lines lasted five more years.

59. The Garstang & Knott End Railway was opened in stages from 1870 in a thinly-populated area. It was intended to carry grain, vegetables and other products, either to Garstang Market or Garstang & Catterall Station (on the L&NW) for onward transmission. Locomotive 'Knott End', purchased in 1908, is pictured, probably near **Knott End** station.

60. The G&KE had a troubled beginning. From about 1908, greater prosperity led the directors to make improvements, and build a final piece of line. At this time, **Nateby** station, three miles west of Garstang, was updated, when an inferior building was replaced by that on the left. The old station house is visible against the crossing.

61. The new building on **Nateby** station incorporated a signal box and waiting room. Later, a rack for water buckets was added to the wall shown. Clearly, the work was still ongoing. The line's passenger services were withdrawn in 1930. Coal, salt, hay, peat and other merchandise were carried until closure in 1950.

62. A novel form of holidaying, which reached a zenith in the 1930s, was the camping coach. The coaches were usually sited near a station. Here, LMS camping coaches, converted from railway carriages, are pictured at Heysham. Holidaymakers were encouraged to book for a week (Saturday to Saturday) or longer.

63. The interior of an LMS camping coach is shown at Heysham. The accommodation usually allowed for six people, with a dining and living room, a kitchen and three bedrooms. Bed and table linen, crockery and cutlery, were included in the tariff. Both these cards were published by B. Matthews of Bradford.